FEB 2 0 2013

Duxbury Free Library

Duxbury , Massachusetts

D1604656

LEIF ERIKSSON

Great Explorers of the World

Viking Explorer of the New World

Cheryl DeFries

Enslow Publishers, Inc.
40 Industrial Road
Box 398
Berkeley Heights, NJ 07922
USA

http://www.enslow.com

Duxbury Free Library

Copyright © 2010 by Enslow Publishers, Inc.

All rights reserved.

No part of this book may be reproduced by any means
without the written permission of the publisher.

Library of Congress Cataloging-in-Publication Data

DeFries, Cheryl L.
Leif Eriksson : Viking explorer of the New World / Cheryl DeFries.
p. cm. — (Great explorers of the world)
Summary: "Examines the life of Viking explorer Leif Eriksson, including his explorations,
his discovery of North America, and his legacy in American history"—Provided by publisher.
Includes bibliographical references and index.
ISBN 978-1-59845-126-9
1. Leiv Eiriksson, d. ca. 1020—Juvenile literature. 2. Explorers—America—Biography—Juvenile
literature. 3. Explorers—Scandinavia—Biography—Juvenile literature. 4. America—Discovery and
exploration—Norse—Juvenile literature. 5. Vikings—Juvenile literature. I. Title.
E105.L47D44 2010
973.1'3092—dc22
[B]
2009044205

Printed in the United States of America

112009 Lake Book Manufacturing, Inc., Melrose Park, IL

10 9 8 7 6 5 4 3 2 1

To Our Readers: We have done our best to make sure all Internet Addresses in this book were active
and appropriate when we went to press. However, the author and the publisher have no control over
and assume no liability for the material available on those Internet sites or on other Web sites they may
link to. Any comments or suggestions can be sent by e-mail to comments@enslow.com or to the address
on the back cover.

♻ Enslow Publishers, Inc., is committed to printing our books on recycled paper. The paper in every
book contains 10% to 30% post-consumer waste (PCW). The cover board on the outside of each book
contains 100% PCW. Our goal is to do our part to help young people and the environment too!

Ship Illustration Used in Chapter Openers: Shutterstock, Inc.

Illustration Credits: © Brian Berry: pp. 74–75; © Brian Enslow: p. 37; © Clipart.com: pp. 20, 39,
44, 46, 52, 65 (top); © Corel Corporation: p. 25, 32 (left), 73; © Courtesy of the U.S. Naval Academy
Museum, painting by Edward Moran (1829–1901): p. 66; © Enslow Publishers, Inc.: pp. 4–5, 62;
© Image of the two carved faces of the Kensington Runestone, from George Flom's short book "The
Kensington Rune-Stone: An Address" (Illinois State Historical Society, 1910): p. 95; © Library of
Congress: pp. 32 (right top and bottom), 65 (bottom), 94; © National Aeronautics and Space
Administration (NASA): p. 10; © Photos.com: pp. 70–71; © Sharon & Claus Ellef: pp. 56–57;
© Sheena Majewski: pp. 12–13; © Shutterstock, Inc: pp. 15–16, 24, 27, 30, 93; © The Art Gallery
Collection / Alamy: p. 54; © Wikimedia: pp. 51, 82–83; @The United States Treasury Department:
p. 90.

Cover Photo: © Shutterstock: Bust of Leif Eriksson (Dedicated by the Scandinavian Community of
Northeast Ohio)

Contents

Greenland

Iceland

• Reykjavik

Atlantic Ocean

Ireland

L'Anse aux Meadows

Vineland

• Lisbon

= Original Viking Land

= Viking Settlements

----→ = Viking Trade or Exploration Routes

Norwegion Sea

Scandinavia

Oslo

Baltic Sea

Britain

Constantinople

Bysantium

Africa

Chapter 1

WHO DISCOVERED NORTH AMERICA?

It was only about fifty years ago when historians gave the credit for the discovery of North America to the explorer, Christopher Columbus. He was recognized as the first to discover North America when he arrived in 1492. However, this claim now has been challenged because of evidence found since 1960.

About A.D. 1000, according to Icelandic sagas, the Vikings claimed that Leif Eriksson, a Viking explorer, established a settlement he called Vinland somewhere on an island in North America. Many scholars and scientists believe that Vinland is today's village of L'Anse Aux Meadows in Newfoundland, Canada.

For more than a thousand years, no one had found any proof to support the Vikings' claim. How was it possible that something as important as this discovery remained a mystery for so long? The fact is that during the life of Leif Eriksson and this period in Viking history, written records did not exist. Without written information, charts, or maps, this claim remained nothing more than just a story.

Leif Eriksson

A Viking Explorer's Discoveries Lost in History

Leif Eriksson's discoveries and conquests escaped recorded history because at the time most people could not read or write. Viking history and information, such as names, explorations, dates, battles, births, and deaths, were recorded as sagas, oral stories passed down from generation to generation. Without written records, much of Leif Eriksson's life remains a mystery.

Often written records and written details were recorded many years after an event took place.[1] This meant that the details might have been changed over time.[2] Names, for instance, would often be spelled as they sounded. So the same person might be known by several names in a recounting of a historical happening. For example, Leif Eriksson's name is spelled many ways throughout history: Leifur Eiriksson, Leiv Eiriksson, Leif Ericson, Leif Eriksson.

Although the Vikings did not keep written records, their victims and enemies often did. Much of the information that exists today about them comes from three sources. One source originates from the European nations, which received, reported, and recorded the brutality of the Viking warriors and when events happened. The second source of information comes directly from the Vikings through their many legends, sagas, poems,

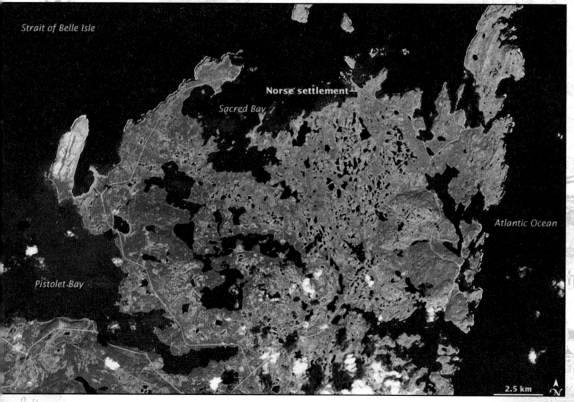

L'Anse aux Meadows as seen from space in a NASA image

and stories. The third source of information comes from researchers who study Viking history and from archaeologists who study the artifacts left behind by the Vikings, such as runes, picture stones, and wood carvings.[3]

L'ANSE AUX MEADOWS DISCOVERED

In 1960, a Norwegian explorer and writer by the name of Helge Ingstad and his wife, Anne Strine

Ingstad, an archaeologist, began to rewrite history. They found an area on a 1670 Icelandic map, which got them excited. Both of them felt the region could be Vinland, the settlement of Leif Eriksson, the place mentioned in the Icelandic sagas.

The map revealed an area called "Promontorium Winlandiae."[4] This area was located in what today is called Newfoundland, Canada. When the Ingstads arrived in Newfoundland, they asked the local people if there were any unusual ruins in the area. They were told about a place called "the Indian camp."[5] A local resident, George Decker, took them to an overgrown area with bumps and ridges.[6] The Ingstads felt that they might be looking at grass-covered ridges, similar to ancient Viking ruins in Greenland and Iceland. They were hopeful that this area would reveal some Viking artifacts and prove that the ancient Vikings had been there.

The Ingstads gathered an international team of archaeologists from the United States, Norway, Iceland, and Sweden to help them excavate the area. The team worked on locating and identifying objects from the site. They worked on this project between 1961 and 1964 and again during 1966 and 1968.[7] The Ingstads' hunch paid off. They found an ancient Viking village called, L'Anse Aux

Meadows, which is located on the northern tip of the island of Newfoundland, Canada.

EXCAVATION BRINGS SUCCESS

During the excavation, the team discovered the remains of eight wood buildings. A few of the buildings were dwellings. Others were workshops used for carpentry, boat repair, and iron works. The team felt that sod and turf may have originally covered the walls and roofs of the buildings

A reconstructed house at L'Anse aux Meadows on the coast of Newfoundland as it might have looked around the year 1000.

as it was a common practice at that time because of the lack of available timber.

Many artifacts were also found in the area. These included a bronze fastening pin, a soapstone spindle whorl used to make yarn or thread for weaving or knitting, a bone knitting needle, a whetstone used to sharpen blades on weapons and tools, and a stone oil lamp.[8] Some of the items such as spindle whorls and knitting needles were tools used by women. Therefore, the team felt

A fastening pin for a cloak can be seen in the upper right-hand portion of this photograph. These items of jewelry were part of the Cuerdale hoard, the loot or bounty of Viking raiders.

that some of the settlers must have been women. Food remains found included butternuts, which is puzzling, because they do not grow where they were found. Historians think the Vikings may have traveled further south to obtain the butternuts.[9] Several years after the Ingstads were finished excavating, the caretakers of the site, Park Canada, excavated the village again. They researched the area from 1973 to 1976 and again later on.[10] The Park Canada excavation uncovered other artifacts, including a bronze pin with a ring-shaped head similar to the ones that the Vikings used to fasten their cloaks, a loom weight, another spindle whorl, a bone needle, jasper fire starters, pollen, seeds, and more butternuts.

DATING OF L'ANSE AUX MEADOWS

In 2000, scraps of worked wood were found at L'Anse Aux Meadows. A test called radiocarbon dating was performed to determine the age of the wood. A radiocarbon test can correctly date an item as old as fifty thousand years. The artifacts tested from L'Anse Aux Meadows were dated to around A.D. 1000.[11] This conclusion was reached because the buildings and artifacts from L'Anse Aux Meadows were similar to buildings and objects found at other ancient Viking sites in Greenland and Iceland from around A.D. 1000.

L'ANSE AUX MEADOWS HONORED

When the teams were finished with their research, they buried the artifacts exactly where they found them. A layer of white sand was placed over the area and then the site was covered with fresh turf. The burial was done for the long-term preservation and protection of the artifacts.

In 1977, Canada designated L'Anse Aux Meadows a National Historic Site and it was included in the World Heritage List. On September 8, 1978, L'Anse Aux Meadows was recognized by the United Nations Educational, Scientific and Cultural Organization (UNESCO) and designated as a World Heritage Site. L'Anse Aux Meadows is the first cultural site in the world to receive this designation.[12]

Chapter 2

Leif Eriksson's Family Tree

No one knows the exact date of Leif Eriksson's birth, but we do know that he was probably born in Iceland and how he got his name. A custom that existed during Leif's life was that each child's last name was based on the father's first name in combination with "son" for a boy and "dottir" for a girl. When Leif's father, Erik the Red, named the son who would later become an explorer, he called him "Leif Eriksson," meaning, "Erik's son."[1]

Leif was born into a family of explorers, murderers, and outlaws who were known for many things, including their bad tempers. The bloodline of Leif Eriksson can be traced back to the Vikings who lived or escaped from Norway, Iceland, and Greenland during the Viking Age. Many of Leif's ancestors fled punishment because they had committed crimes.

ICELAND AND ITS IMPORTANCE TO LEIF

According to historians, in the ninth century at about the same time, two explorers landed on the shores of Iceland. One was a relative of Leif's, his great-granduncle

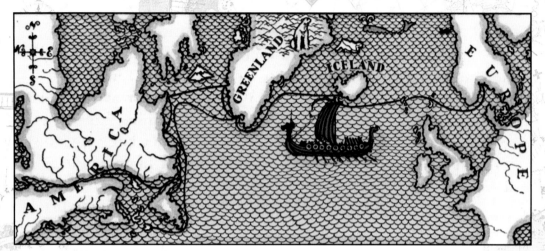

The Vikings sailed to and settled in Iceland, Greenland, and parts of North America.

Naddod, a Norwegian explorer and Viking raider, and the other was Gardar Svavarsson, a Swedish explorer. Their discovery of Iceland helped save the life of Leif' Eriksson's grandfather Thorvald Asvaldsson.

THE DISCOVERY OF ICELAND

Iceland was too far away and too treacherous for most European sailors to explore. Fogs were frequent, and the sailors who used the sun to guide them could easily end up sailing in the wrong direction.

According to historians, Naddod of Norway and Gardar Svavarsson of Sweden probably landed on the shores of Iceland, an island, by accident about A.D. 861. Naddod was trying to escape from his enemies and reach the Faeroe Islands, but his ship was blown off course. Rather than follow the coastline of the island, Naddod beached his ship and climbed to the top of a mountain to see if there were any signs of human settlement, but he did not see anything. Before continuing his voyage to the Faeroe Islands, he named the island Snael-and, meaning "Snowland," because of the snow and snow-covered mountains.

About the same time, a Swedish explorer named Gardar Svavarsson also discovered Iceland. He was on his way to the Hebrides Islands on the west coast of Scotland to collect his wife's inheritance. A storm drove Gardar off course and took him into the North Atlantic Ocean. He sailed on in a southwestern direction until he came into a huge bay rimmed with mountains and volcanoes.

Summer was ending, and Gardar knew that the harsh northern winter would soon prevent him from sailing any farther. He anchored his ship in a natural harbor and built a house for the winter, which he named Husavik, meaning "House Bay."

When spring came, Gardar hoisted sail and continued his voyage home to Sweden. He spoke highly of this island and he named it Gardarsholm.

FLOKI'S VILGERDARSON VOYAGE

About A.D. 867, a third Viking explorer named Floki Vilgerdarson set out from Norway. It was his intention to find this new land in the west. He liked what he heard about Snaeland and intended to settle permanently there. To help him find Snaeland, he brought ravens on his voyage. The raven that flew away and never came back had found land. This gave Floki the nickname "Raven-Floki."

Following Naddod's sailing directions, Floki reached Snaeland safely and built a building on the far side of the great bay called Breidafjord. There was pasture for the livestock, a fjord full of fish and seals, and summer days for growing food. Unfortunately, Floki and his crewmates realized too late that summer would not last forever. Winter came, and snow and ice covered the green pastures, and their Norwegian cattle all starved to death.

When spring finally came, it was cold and wet. Climbing a mountain to survey the countryside, the unhappy Floki Vilgerdarson saw only a long fjord, choked with drifting ice. Giving up thoughts of a permanent settlement, Floki and his crew tried to head home to Norway, but unexpected storms blew their ship back to shore. When they finally made their way home, Floki had nothing but bad things to say about Iceland. He gave the island a third name, changing it from Snowland to Island, meaning Iceland.[2]

Within fifty years, however, from A.D. 870 to A.D. 930, between five thousand and fifteen thousand settlers, mostly from western Norway and the Norse colonies in the British Isles, settled the vast island.

Ari Thorgilsson the Learned (1067–1118), an Icelandic historian, recorded the names of 430 settlers in his Landnámabók, *The Book of Settlements*. The Norse used the land to raise stock and settle farms. They created the first overseas European colonial society governed by laws and courts. Later Icelanders claimed that their ancestors had immigrated to escape the tyranny of King Harald Finehair (880–930). In 930, the leading chieftains established a national Althing, the parliament, which met each summer. This free republic proved a remarkable success in self-government.[3]

🌐 Iceland

Iceland is a plateau built up by volcanoes, snowfields, and glaciers. It is almost forty thousand square miles and about three hundred miles across. In some places, travel across the middle of the island is impossible.

The greatest glacier in Iceland is Vatnajokull. Its snowfield covers nearly three thousand square miles. Such glaciers are hundreds of feet deep and never melt completely. Iceland also has a number of active volcanoes. Lava flowing from volcanoes

The trail of dust is the telltale sign of an approaching car in the barren, empty Sprengisandur Highlands of Iceland, with the Vatnajokull glacier and volcano in the background

can melt the glaciers and cause great destruction to the land, and the ash of erupting volcanoes can cause sickness in animals and humans.

Although Iceland is almost treeless, it has good pastureland. Settlers raised cattle, sheep, and horses. Fish were available for food, but the ability to grow fruits, vegetables, or grains was limited. From the start, Iceland's settlers had to depend on imported food.[4]

The Icelanders were a tough and rugged people and did not want a king to rule them. They wanted to govern themselves under the ancient Germanic assembly known as the Althing. Eventually, the settlers divided Iceland into four quarters, each with its own assembly. After A.D. 930, each assembly would send representatives to a yearly national Althing.

🌐 ICELAND SETTLERS

The *Landnámabók,* or *The Book of Settlements,* tells the stories of some four hundred of Iceland's original settlers, who came with their families, slaves, livestock, and supplies to make new lives for themselves in Iceland. Within sixty years, people claimed all of Iceland's habitable land.

The green fields and mountains of Iceland were the sites for Viking villages. This is Stoknes, Iceland.

Norway, with limited land resources, had trouble supporting an ever-growing population. Like pioneers throughout history, the prospect of owning vast unclaimed lands to the west drew many people to search out the unknown.

Two papal, or religious, documents dated 1053 and 1055, contain some of the earliest details about Iceland's settlement, but for other accounts, there are the Icelandic sagas, events remembered by the Icelanders and passed from generation to generation as oral stories.

● LEIF ERIKSSON'S FAMILY

Thorvald Asvaldsson, Leif Eriksson's grandfather, was born in Norway. In 960, during King Harald Finehair's reign, Thorvald Asvaldsson committed a murder. Because of his crime, he was forced to leave Norway.[5] Asvaldsson took his ten-year-old son, Erik, and left the country.[6] They settled in Iceland and made it their home. Thorvald Asvaldsson died in Iceland around 980.

Erik Thorvaldsson, Leif's father, was born in Norway around 950 and died in Greenland between 1000 and 1005. Like Leif, his father's name has many different spellings, but today he is known as "Erik the Red." Some say he got his nickname because of his blazing red hair and beard; others suggest he received the name because of his fiery temper.

Following the death of his father, Erik moved to another part of Iceland. There he had one daughter, Freydis, before he married Thjodhild, Leif's mother. After her marriage to Thorvaldsson, Thjodhild bore him three sons, Torstein, Torvald, and Leif.

SCHOOL AWAY FROM HOME

In the tradition of the Vikings, Leif did not grow up with his family. During the Viking Age, families sent their young boys away to be educated and learn skills. When Leif was eight, he moved in with a teacher named Thyrker who was put in charge of Leif's education. Leif's teacher was from Germany. Erik the Red had captured Thyrker and had taken him back to Iceland but had not made him a slave.

Thyrker taught Leif reading and writing runes, symbols in the ancient Germanic alphabet, which the Scandinavian people spoke. During the Viking Age, the Vikings spoke a Germanic language called "Old Norse."[7] Early Old Norse was written in runes and later the language used the Latin alphabet along with the runes.[8] The Old Norse language is the basis of today's modern Scandinavian languages: Icelandic, Faroese, Norwegian, Danish, and Swedish.[9] Thyrker also taught Leif the Celtic and Russian languages.[10]

Karlevi runic stone on the Swedish island of Oeland with an ancient verse about a Danish Viking chief

For the period that Leif lived with his teacher and friend, he learned how to farm, use weapons, sail, hunt, and fish. When Leif was not learning, he and his friends would watch the ships come into the harbor and listen to the stories of the sailors. With each story, Leif yearned more and more for the day to come when he would be old enough to go to sea and explore the unknown.

LEIF ERIKSSON RETURNS HOME

By the time Leif reached the age of twelve, Viking society considered him a man, as he had mastered many skills.[11] When his education with Thyrker was completed, Leif returned to his father's house. He saw that there were many changes. The area around his home was larger. The herds of cattle, horses, pigs, and sheep had multiplied, and there were new houses and more slaves.

ICELANDIC SOCIETY AND THE ALTHING

After Leif returned home, Erik the Red had to go to the Althing, the lawmaking assembly. He took Leif along with him. In Erik's day, it was up to the Icelandic families to enforce the laws.

Icelandic families had to carry out the policing and punishment themselves. Iceland had no cities or towns, and the settlements were isolated farmsteads. Such farmsteads might have family units of perhaps several hundred people and made up

The Iceland Althing met annually from the year 930 at Thingvellir or Parliament Plains. The open-air site is set before a natural wall of lava.

the society. A chieftain, also called a "godi," controlled the local society and acted as the go-between among the landholders. The settlers no longer had a king and their pattern of government was much simpler. The Althing sealed marriages and business contracts at legislative meetings. The "law-speaker" was elected for a three-year term. He stood on the "Law Rock" and recited the law from memory, one-third of it for each year of his term.

At the Law Rock, citizens had the right to have major disputes heard and settlements made. Icelanders were generally law-abiding people, and men and women, except slaves, could speak, testify, and settle disputes according to the Norse laws.

ERIK THE RED'S EXILE

After Erik the Red's marriage, he moved to another area of Iceland. During the clearing of his land in Haukadal, two of his slaves accidentally started a landslide on the farm of Valthjof, a neighbor. A relative of Valthjof, Eyiolf the Foul, killed the slaves. Erik was very angry when he discovered that his slaves were killed because of an accident. The men argued and Erik killed Valthjof and Eyiolf the Foul.[12]

The families of the slain men found Erik guilty and banished him from Haukadal. He stayed in

31

The Viking helmet was important protection during fighting.

A Viking warrior fought with a broad two-edged blade made of iron and steel.

Iceland, but moved from the area. During the winter, he loaned a neighbor, Thorgest, tools, which Erik considered family heirlooms. When the neighbor would not return them, Erik and some men went to get the tools back. As they carried the tools away, Thorgest ran after them. During the fight that erupted, Erik murdered the man's sons and some supporters.[13]

NORSEMEN'S DEADLY WEAPONS

The ancient Norse laws said that every able-bodied man should own and carry weapons. However, often in the heat of an argument, the weapons would be used. Although killing a person was a serious matter in Iceland, Icelandic law during the Viking Age allowed many legal reasons for killing a person. For example, during Leif Eriksson's lifetime, when an insult was made, the people of Iceland allowed one person to kill another person. They wanted a person to keep a civil tongue in his head when speaking to an armed person, or be prepared to pay the consequences.[14]

BLOOD MONEY

During Leif Eriksson's lifetime, a payment or fine often settled the trouble caused by a killing. The Althing could suggest that the killer's family pay a fine to the victim's family. Depending on how valuable the victim was, the Althing might also suggest the amount the victim's family should receive. If the amount of money was acceptable to both families, the issue was then legally settled.

All the members of the killer's family, including distant relatives, had to chip in to pay the amount of money that the Althing had declared. Every member of the victim's family received some of the money. This is where the expression "blood money" comes from.

However, the victim's family did not have to accept the money, no matter how large the amount. They could decide that the killer or some other family member had to die in order to see justice done. If they decided to take a life instead of money, then the victim's family had to seek its own revenge and do its own killing. Sometimes two families might seek vengeance from each other repeatedly. This had led to blood feuds that lasted for years.

BANISHMENT

Sometimes the Althing would banish someone involved in a blood feud. This meant that for a certain amount of time, the Althing could take away from the guilty person the protection of the laws that governed killing. A banished person became an outlaw, and anybody had the right to kill such a person without fear of having to pay a fine or even answering to the outlaw's family.

The banished person did not have to leave home, but the chances of staying alive while under banishment were not good. Most banished Icelanders went into hiding or tried to leave Iceland. Leif's father knew about banishment. He also knew what he needed to do to survive.

This system of justice may seem cruel today. To the Icelanders of the time, killing was not always bad and it seemed sensible. They believed some people deserved to die. It also seemed right to them that the people harmed by a person's death should get something in return, either money or vengeance. What was an unthinkable, unforgivable crime was to kill someone in secret and not announce it right away.

GUILTY OF MANSLAUGHTER

The Althing found that Erik the Red was guilty of manslaughter and a decision was made. As a punishment for the crime of murder, he received banishment. As a newly convicted outlaw, Erik the Red had to leave Iceland quickly and for three years. Staying in Iceland after his conviction meant anyone could have legally killed him.

As Leif grew into manhood, he must have heard the Icelandic laws about killing discussed many times. Not every Icelandic boy had a father and grand-father who had been involved in blood feuds, murder, and banishment. Although Leif Eriksson was born into a hot-tempered, warlike family, no country ever banished him.

ERIK THE RED SAILS WEST

Some time around the early tenth century, Gunn-bjorn Ulfsson was blown off course while sailing to Iceland from Norway. He sighted land about five hundred miles west of Iceland. Gunnbjorn did not step onto the land, but he did give the land the name of Gunnbjarnarsker, meaning Gunnbjorn's skerries, or little islands.

Gunnbjorn Ulfsson told Erik the Red of the land he had sighted west of Iceland. Immediately after Erik's conviction, sometime between 980 and 982, Erik loaded his ship, took his family, some slaves, and food supplies, and said farewell to his country and friends. As he sailed off in search of this new land, little did anyone realize how this new land would save him from a certain fate of death.

ERIK THE RED AND GREENLAND

Erik the Red found the land that Gunnbjorn Ulfs-son had seen. At first glance, the land did not look good to him, but he continued to sail along the coastline for several hundred miles until he reached the southwest side of the island. He found

According to legend, this is the spot where Erik the Red left Iceland.

fjords that he could navigate and plenty of seals and polar bears for food.

Erik decided to settle there, and he hoped that, eventually, if he gave the new land an interesting name, it would attract others to settle there, too. He named it Greenland.

At first, Erik and Leif built a camp. During the early years in Greenland, his father taught Leif how to be a sailor. Throughout the three years Erik spent in banishment in Greenland, he explored the land, and he saw that ice and snow covered half of Greenland.

Erik also found that a small population of Inuits lived on Greenland. The name Inuit, which means "the people" or "real people," comes from a language called Inuit-Inupiaq. The singular of nuit is Inuk, which means person. Dialects of the Inuit-Inupiaq language are spoken by the Inuit in Canada, Greenland, and northern Alaska.

After he completed his three-year banishment, EriK the Red returned home praising Greenland. Many people decided they wanted to move to Greenland with Erik because times were not good in Iceland. There had been a food shortage and the lands were overgrazed. There were almost no trees left for fuel and the building of ships.

According to the *Íslendingabók*, *The Book of Icelanders*, written by Ari Thorgilsson, the "Father of Icelandic history," Erik the Red, led twenty-five ships carrying settlers toward their new home in Greenland. This fleet of ships set out on a journey of more than 750 miles (1200 km). The seas were rough and only about half of the ships reached Greenland. Some ships sank and some ships turned back to Iceland because of the difficulty sailing on the rough seas.

History has credited Erik the Red with discovering Greenland and establishing two settlements there on the western side of Greenland. One was

After he completed his three-year banishment, Erik the Red returned home praising Greenland.

the Eastern Settlement, or Eystribyggd, and the other was the Western Settlement, or Vestribyggd. In an area called, Osterbygd Erik built his estate known as Brattahlid, today's Qassiarsuk, which was the heart of the Eastern Settlement.[15] For the duration of the time Erik lived and developed the settlements in Greenland, he became a very wealthy man and he was greatly respected.

LEIF AND THE POLAR BEAR

According to unsubstantiated stories, when Leif was about sixteen, he saw a young polar bear on a piece of thick ice. He wanted to capture the bear, but there was a strong current between the ice and land. Using the knowledge of the sea, which his father had taught him, Leif went upstream from the polar bear. He then let the current carry his boat into the ice. After capturing the bear, he used the same method to get back to land. This impressed the people watching on shore. Some stories about Leif and the bear have claimed he tamed the bear and made the bear his pet.

LEIF ERIKSSON AS A YOUNG MAN

Many of the sagas differ on facts, but they all seem to agree that Leif Eriksson was known for his fairness and honesty. Some stories say Leif inherited his sense of adventure and desire for exploration from his father. Other descriptions of Leif state that "[h]e was a big strapping fellow, handsome to look at, thoughtful in all things." In addition, Leif was described as "wise and magnanimous."

Both Erik and Leif were Viking explorers who desired, in part, to attain land for the wealth and power that might come from it. Unlike some of his relatives, however, Leif wanted to leave Greenland in search of new lands and new resources for the people of Greenland.

INDIGENOUS PEOPLE OF GREENLAND

The *Íslendingabók* also states that the Viking settlers found human dwellings, fragments of skin boats, and stone artifacts like those belonging to the Skraeling of Vinland. *Skraeling* is the name the Norse Greenlanders gave to the Thule, the indigenous people they encountered in Greenland.

Archaeologists refer to the people who left these traces as the Dorset people, naming them after the place on Baffin Island where their remains were first recognized. They had been living in the Arctic for hundreds of years, along with other groups. By the time the Vikings arrived, the onset of warmer conditions was encouraging the Dorset people to leave Greenland. It may be that the early Viking Greenlanders and the Dorset

people rarely, if ever, came face-to-face around the settled areas during the Viking Age.

VIKING SHIPS

The Vikings were very skilled shipbuilders for their time. Their cargo ships were used to carry goods for trade. They also had warships called longships. These longships were about sixty-five to ninety-five feet long. The Vikings made their ships better by adding a keel. A keel is a long, narrow piece of wood attached to the bottom of a ship. This helped the ship stay straight in the water and made it faster. Longships had fifteen to thirty pairs of rowers and sailed well in calm or stormy weather. Their prow, or front end, of a Viking longship sometimes had a snake or dragon head carved from wood.

Even after the Vikings charted the sea routes, sea voyages, particularly in the fall and winter, remained dangerous. Fierce winds, very rough and treacherous seas, fog, rain, or snow could contribute to the sinking of a ship. But the Vikings also learned to use the weather to their advantage. In the cover of fog, for example, they could withdraw, avoid, or hide from their enemies.

VIKING RAIDS

Some Vikings used their ships and sailing skills to raid villages, rob and burn churches, and steal

WHO WERE THE VIKINGS?

Viking is a modern word that refers to the Nordic-speaking people from southern Scandinavian countries who raided, traded, looted, and settled in Europe and the British Isles.[16] Many historians believe the Viking Age was during the years from 750 to 1066 and was composed of a mixture of people and cultures from Norway, Sweden, and Denmark. Scandinavian Vikings are known as Norsemen, Normans, or Norse.

Although notorious for their fearsome Viking raids, not all Vikings were barbarians. Most did not plunder or terrorize their neighbors; many Vikings spent only a portion of their time on raids, which nearly all occurred in the summer months. During the rest of the year, these warriors remained at home, working their farms and fishing. Many of the Viking people made their living as merchants, seamen, shipbuilders, artists, poets, storytellers, singers, or traders.

Some Vikings raised goats, sheep, and cows for food and others raised animals to work the farm and help with everyday tasks. The Vikings used horses to help them with farming and to load ships with supplies for voyages or merchandise for trading. Others were skillful with their hands, creating items needed by people. This covered a range of items from jewelry to deadly weapons. A number of Vikings earned respect and honor as explorers and discoverers of new lands. Many of them became very wealthy from their discoveries. In order to fulfill their ambitions, these men had to become skilled at navigating and sailing on rough seas and building reliable and seaworthy ships to enable them to reach and return from distant lands safely.

Viking longship

from wealthy homes. Their slender, swift boats descended upon coastal villages, churches, homes, and monasteries, stealing everything valuable that they could carry. Before the village people or monks knew what was happening, the Vikings would swarm upon them, swords in hand. The monasteries were the raiders' favorite targets because much of the country's wealth was in their treasure rooms.[17]

Throughout this time, the Vikings also made raids where they murdered and captured people living along the coasts or inland on rivers in Europe. The Vikings used fear and threats to control their victims. These fierce and violent warriors burned buildings, destroyed towns, captured land, and devastated families. Residents were murdered or kidnapped and taken as prisoners to be slaves. The Vikings would take the captives back to their home country or sell them as slaves to others. In time, much of Europe feared the Vikings.

Today, we see pictures of Vikings wearing helmets with horns or wings. The Viking never wore this type of helmet. During the Viking Age, they wore a type of helmet called a *spangenhelm*.[18] It was made of iron and iron bands, and a nose guard was attached to the main helmet. Perhaps the stories about wings and horns on helmets

Viking warriors enjoyed fighting. They were bold and adventurous, but they were also brutal and fearsome. They murdered women and children as well as men. What they did not steal, they burned. The Vikings created such terror in the hearts of other Europeans that a special prayer for protection was offered in the churches: "God, deliver us from the fury of the Northmen."

added to the Viking tales and made them look as frightening as their true raiding reputation.

FINDING NEW LANDS

By the time Leif Eriksson was a young man, the Viking raids were less frequent. Many Vikings were more interested in finding new lands for their growing population than in seeking out new places to pillage.

Sailing conditions from Norway to Iceland were treacherous. It is around 600 miles (965.606 kilometers) from Bergen, the main port of Norway, to the eastern shores of Iceland. From Sweden, Vikings sailed the rivers of eastern Europe that lead to the Black Sea and to the Middle East. The location of these Scandinavian countries gave the Vikings fast access to the seas.

The travels of Norwegian Vikings lead them west to settle Iceland in 874, and still further west to settle in Greenland about a hundred years later. By the year 1000, they had even reached and set up at least one camp in North America, almost five hundred years before Christopher Columbus's arrival in 1492. Among the reasons for their explorations was the Vikings' desire for wealth, power, and adventure.

47

Chapter 3
Leif Eriksson's First Voyage

When Leif Eriksson was twenty-four, he set out on what was his first voyage to Norway as the ship's captain. He was bringing gifts to King Olaf in Norway. Leif took a crew of fourteen and his former teacher, Thyrker, on the voyage. Although the journey usually took two days, because of the slow winds it took five days before they sighted any land.

When the crew saw land, they wanted to go ashore, but Leif would not let them. They continued sailing for days until they sighted some small islands, the Hebrides. Then Leif realized they had sailed farther south than he had intended.

The day Leif arrived on the Hebrides, a storm came up and he and his crew could not leave the Hebrides for a month. During this time, Leif stayed in the house of the lord of the island and met the lord's daughter, Thorgunna, and he fell in love with her. Thorgunna wanted to go with Leif when he sailed, but he refused to take her because he felt that her relatives might try to stop them from leaving together, and he had a mission to deliver the gifts to King Olaf.

Before Leif left, Thorgunna told him that she was going to have a baby. Leif gave Thorgunna gifts: a gold ring, a belt made of walrus tusks, and a "wadmal mantl," a cape made of woolen cloth. Thorgunna gave birth to a son who she named Thorkell, or Thorgils, Leifsson. Eventually, she went to Greenland with her son. He died young and was Leif Eriksson's only known child.

LEIF ERIKSSON BECOMES A CHRISTIAN

When Leif Eriksson arrived in the city of Nidaros, today called Trondheim, Norway, he was greeted by many people and taken to meet King Olaf Tryggvason. The king was impressed with Leif's journey and he asked many questions about Greenland and its people. King Olaf then invited Leif to spend the winter with him in his royal court.

Leif told the king that he planned to return home to Greenland in the spring. Upon hearing of his plans, the king told Leif he had a special mission for him to carry out. Honored by the king's request, Leif listened to the king's proposal.

King Olaf began by explaining that once he, too, had worshipped pagan gods as Eriksson, his crew, and other Vikings did. As a pagan, he had not belonged to any religious group but had prayed to many pagan gods such as Odin, the god of wisdom, wars, and death, and Thor, the god of

The Vikings had many gods and goddesses. Their most important one was Odin who was the god of battle.

Thor was one of Odin's sons. He was the god of the thunder and lightning. He drove a chariot, which caused thunder, and created lightning with his hammer.

thunder. Like Leif, King Olaf believed that the different pagan gods ruled peoples' lives.

Then one day, the king said, a plague struck Norway and many people died. King Olaf told Eriksson how he had turned away from the pagan gods and began to worship Jesus Christ. The king spoke about the power of the Christian faith and how Christ had conquered the pagan gods and sent them to the underworld.

In A.D. 995, while in England, King Olaf and his men were baptized Christians by Alphege, Bishop of Windsor, who performed the ceremony at Andover, England. After he became a Christian, the king said, the plague stopped.[1] When King Olaf returned to Norway, he convinced most of his people to convert to the Christian religion.

Now the king wanted Leif to help him convert the people in Greenland to Christianity. King Olaf told Leif that his followers must convert to Christianity. The king felt it was so important that if they did not become Christians, they would be physically harmed, banished, or worse yet, executed. This same choice was offered to Leif: convert or die. The king gave Leif two weeks to decide if he would convert, and Leif took the entire time to decide. Leif finally decided that the Vikings had so many pagan gods to pray to that there was enough room to add the one Christian god, so he allowed the king to baptize him and his crew.

When spring came, Leif was ready to carry Christianity home to the people in Greenland. The king wanted Leif to take a priest with him so that the people could learn all about Christianity. King Olaf also asked Leif to help the priest convince the people to convert to Christianity. When Leif and his crew were ready to leave Norway, the king wished Leif Eriksson good luck. The king also gave

This amulet in the shape of Thor's hammer also incorporates Christian symbolism (the Cross). For many years the newly converted Vikings did not fully accept Christianity and continued to worship the old gods alongside the new faith.

Leif many gifts, including Haig and Haigie, two Scottish slaves.

Although Leif wanted to please King Olaf, he knew it would not be easy to convert the Greenlanders to Christianity because of their strong beliefs in pagan traditions, myths, and legends. Before people could write, knowledge was shared orally, and each time someone repeated a story, it changed a little. From these ever-changing tales, myths and legends were born. They included stories that explained the origin of life and tales of superhuman beings with special godlike powers that could affect one's life. So they prayed to pagan gods to ensure their good will.

LEIF ERIKSSON ARRIVES HOME SAFELY

At first, Erik the Red was happy to see his son again and was proud of his son's accomplishments when Leif returned from Norway. Leif had brought honor to his family by serving King Olaf.

Erik, however, was not happy to see that his son had a Christian priest with him, and he referred to the priest as a trickster, a fraud. Erik did not like the idea that his son and the priest wanted his people to become Christians. Even though his father did not like what he was doing, Leif kept his word to the king. He helped teach the people in Greenland his new Christian beliefs.

The ruins of a medieval church mark the site of Brattahlid, where Erik the Red settled in 983 when he established the first Norse colony in Greenland.

However, Leif did not want to anger his father so he continued the old pagan ways of worship, but he also added the Christian god to his prayers. He felt that because the Norse faith had many gods there was room for one more.

Leif's mother, Thjodhild, felt differently about converting to Christianity. She listened to her son and the priest. Around the year 1000, she gave up her pagan beliefs and became a Christian. She liked her new religion. After her baptism, she began talking about building a church at Bratahlid, their estate.[2] Because she was very dedicated to her new faith, Thjodhild asked her husband to have a church built for worship. Grudgingly, Erik built a small church at Brattahlid. She was very proud of her new church and named it Thjodhild's Church. It was the first church built in Greenland.

Leif and the priest went from farm to farm for many months. By the spring, enough of the people in Greenlanders had agreed to become Christians to satisfy King Olaf's wishes. Then the priest continued on in his work converting people to Christianity by himself.

Many people in Greenland did not want to give up their ways, but they felt had no choice. The Greenlanders were afraid to make the king angry. It was easier to become a Christian than to become an enemy of the king and be killed.

As a result, the religion of King Olaf of Norway spread throughout the Norse countries. He stated that the old pagan ways and beliefs should be discarded and replaced with the beliefs of Christianity. The king sent the son of Count Willibald of Saxony, Thangbrand, and a famous warrior named Gudlief Arason, to Iceland. He wanted them to convert Icelanders to Christianity. These men met with hostility, but they continued in their quest to make the country of Iceland a Christian country.[3] The Althing ratified the conversion of Iceland to Christianity in 1000. After the Viking Age, Christian beliefs replaced most of the pagan beliefs.

Chapter 4
A Major Discovery

One day, when Leif Eriksson was at a harbor in Greenland watching the boats, he saw an old ship rowing into the harbor very slowly. He knew that this ship belonged to Bjarni Herjulfsson, who had been away for more than a year.

After the ship landed, Bjarni told the villagers he had gone to Iceland to spend the winter with his father. When he arrived in Eyar, Iceland, he found that his father had gone to Greenland with Erik the Red.[1] Bjarni did not unload his cargo but set sail to Greenland in 986. He was sailing between Iceland and Greenland when a strong storm caused him to go off course. Fog had covered the North Star, which Bjarni used to chart his course. Because of the fog, he could not navigate. Bjarni and his crew sailed for days until they spotted land.

It was not Greenland, where they had been heading. The land did not have glaciers covering the coast. This land was green with trees. They kept on sailing and found some more land that was level and forest covered, but they did not stop there either. Another island they saw was rocky

with glaciers, and it had no plant life. Bjarni said
that although they spotted three different land-
masses, they never stepped foot on them because
they were anxious to sail back to Greenland.

Leif listened to Bjarni's story of how he got lost.
For many years they talked about these lands
Bjarni had seen but had not been curious enough
to explore.

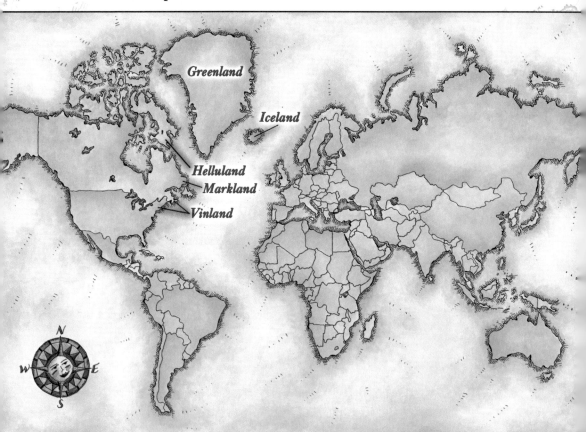

Erikkson sailed west from Greenland to seek a land that had been
sighted by Bjarni Herjulfsson. According to the sagas, Erikkson and his
crew first landed at Helluland (Flat Rock Land). He then sailed farther
south to a region he called Markland (Forestland). He continued south
and went ashore at a place he called it Vinland (Wineland).

For fifteen years, Leif did nothing about the lands that Bjarni had sighted.[2] Finally, Leif decided to search for these lands to the west. Historians believe the lands that Bjarni saw are the present-day Newfoundland, Markland, and Helluland, Canada. They also feel he and his crew were the first Europeans to see North America. However, because there is no record to prove that Bjarni Herjulfsson and his crew stepped onto the land, they were not credited with the discovery of North America.

LEIF DISCOVERS NORTH AMERICA

In the summer of 1000, after Leif returned from his visit with King Olaf, he heard "much talk about voyages of discovery." Erik and other settlers in Greenland had set up farming and hunting communities, but they were held back from developing them further because they needed wood. Greenland had no timber larger than small brush. The settlers had to depend on turf and driftwood for building and fuel.[3] Leif hoped that one of the lands that Bjarni saw might yield the timber so desperately needed by Greenland settlers, so he decided to buy Bjarni's ship and search for the lands Bjarni had talked about.

Leif planned to take his father with him on the journey. Leif and his crew considered Erik the Red to be a lucky charm and thought that if he sailed with them, he would bring their journey success. Erik was aging and he was very comfortable in Greenland. He really did not want to go to sea, but he decided to please his son and sail with Leif and his crew.

When the day arrived for Leif and his father to depart, there was an accident. Erik was thrown from his horse, injuring his foot. Erik considered this a bad omen, so he decided not to go on the voyage.

Leif set sail with Thyrker and a crew of thirty-five. He decided to search for the lands to the west that Bjarni Herjulfsson had seen, except he made the journey in reverse. After sailing north along the western coast of Greenland, he sailed west for several hundred miles. Finally, he sighted land.

The crew cast anchor, launched a small boat, and went ashore. They were disappointed in what they saw. The land was a slab of rock, which stretched from the sea to the mountains of ice. There was no grass and almost no vegetation. Leif named it Helluland (Flat Rock Land). Today, historians believe he discovered Baffin Island, a rocky island with few trees, which lies south of the Arctic Circle.

Disappointed with Helluland as a source of timber, Leif continued sailing south and found more land. Once ashore, Leif found it to be flat with white beaches and thick trees. He named the land Markland, which in the Norse language means "forestland" or "borderland." According to a Norse epic poem, the *Saga of the Greenlanders*, Leif and his crew cut down trees and took them to Greenland. When Viking settlements were excavated, birch trees were found. Perhaps these trees were the ones from Markland. Today historians believe that Markland is the eastern coast of

These people are pretending to be Vikings in a recreated longhouse.

Main photo: Eriksson and his men spent the winter in a longhouse like this.

Leif Eriksson makes landfall in Vinland.

Labrador, Canada, which lies in the heavily forested area in the Northern Hemisphere.

DISCOVERY OF VINLAND

Leif continued to sail but this time in a southeast direction. He discovered more land, and it was green and lush. The crew returned to their ship and then sailed into an inlet and ran aground. After the tide came in, they guided the ship into a lake and cast anchor. A base camp was established and it was called Leifsbudir meaning "Leif's Camp."[4] Leif decided that he and his crew would spend the winter there. They built at least one large house, a longhouse, for the winter. The Old Norse longhouses measured 55 feet wide by 70 feet long (16.764 meters by 21.336 meters). The house had a central hall, with a fireplace. Around the central hall were six to eight smaller rooms.[5]

In this new land, both the rivers and lakes had plenty of fish, such as salmon, and the fish were bigger than any the Vikings had ever seen. There were thick forests covering the land. The rich pastures were perfect for the cattle they had brought. The herds would not need to have hay or straw over the winter because the grass did not die from winter frost or snow. However, the winter was very different from the winters in Iceland or Norway. The winter was milder, and unlike Greenland and Iceland, the days and night were equal in length.

Once they had built a permanent camp, Leif divided the men into two groups. One group of men would stay at the house and the other would explore the land and report back. Leif instructed the crew not to go so far that they could not return to the house at night. On one of these exploring trips, Thyrker did not return. Leif and some of the men searched for him. When they found Thyrker the next morning, he was so excited that he was talking in German, his native tongue. He explained to Leif that he had found grapes on this land. Thyrker knew they were grapes as they grew in Germany, his homeland. Since grapes did not grow in Greenland, this was an important find.

The men found three products that were unknown in Greenland. They were grapes, "self-sown wheat," perhaps Indian corn, wild grass with a wheat-like head or wild rice, and white or canoe birch. Leif planned to make a profit in Greenland from his cargo of timber and grapes. [6] He ordered his men to load grapes and timber onto the boat, and then they settled in for the winter.

Leif called this land Vinland, which means Wineland or Pastureland. Some historians say the name Vinland does not refer to the wild grapes. Instead, they say it was named for the grasses that were important to feed the livestock. Many historians believe Leif's Vinland was discovered at L'Anse Aux Meadows, in Newfoundland, Canada.

When spring came, Leif and his crew were ready to go. They set sail from Vinland with a ship filled with timber they needed in Greenland and grapes.

LEIF THE LUCKY

On the return trip from Vinland to Greenland, Leif saw some people in the distance on a skerry, a small rocky island usually too small to live on. Their ship was damaged and her crew was stranded. Leif's crew tacked toward the skerry while lowering the sails. Once they cast the anchor, Leif and Thyrker and some crew rowed to the skerry. When they reached the skerry, Thyrker asked who the leader of the party was. One of the stranded men said his name was Thori and he was a Norseman. Thori asked Leif his name and when Leif replied, Thori had another question. "Art thou the son of Erik the Red of Brattahlid?' Leif said he was and he would take them and their cargo to Greenland.

After traveling a great distance, Leif arrived in Greenland with his crew and the fifteen ship-wrecked people he had rescued from the skerry. This included Thori and his wife, Gudrid.[7] Leif put them up at his house, and he helped to find homes for the rest of the crew. For his good deed in rescu-ing the shipwrecked people, he received the cargo and timber from the damaged ship as a reward.

Sixty-three

The final stop in Vikings' expansion across the Atlantic Ocean was North America. The name Vineland probably came from the Old Norse word "vin," meaning field or meadow.

Leif became a hero to his people. Between the cargo and a reward, he became a very rich man. The people began calling him "Leif the Lucky."

Leif probably wanted to return to Vinland, but when his father died, Leif took over running the colony in Greenland.

ERIK THE RED DIES

Around 1003, after Leif returned from North America, Erik the Red died during an epidemic of illness among the colonists. When Erik died, Leif received his father's title, "Paramount Chief of Greenland," as well as his father's estate, Bratthahlid. Although he took over as chieftain in Greenland, Leif still owned the property he had discovered in Vinland. This meant he had to give permission for any expeditions to Vinland. It also meant that he would receive part of the ship's cargo as tax.[8]

Leif probably expected to return to Vinland, but there is no proof that he ever did. Although Leif was a powerful and important man in his time, historians do not know how Leif died or even where he is buried. However, it was probably not in a battle. No one knows if Leif had a Viking funeral or a Christian burial. Although there are different stories about Leif's son, Torkell, many scholars say the title of "Paramount Chief of Greenland" was passed to him when Leif died.

A VIKING FUNERAL

Although historians do not know anything about Leif's death, they do know about Viking funerals, particularly a funeral for someone as important a leader as Leif Eriksson. As a tribute to a man's important position, the Vikings sometimes burned their dead leaders in ship burials. Most Viking funerals, however, took place on land. As part of the burial ritual, the dead Viking's last resting place was in a boat, but the boat and the body

Vikings often put stones around a grave. These stones were often placed in the shape of an oval, a triangle, or a ship.

OSEBERG SHIP

Displayed in the Viking Ship Musuem in Oslo, Norway, are three Viking burial vessels that were excavated near the Oslofjord. One of the ships, the Oseberg, dates back to the ninth century. The Oseberg, shown on the facing page, was built around 815–820 A.D. and was used as a sailing vessel for many years before it was used as a burial ship for a prominent woman who died in 834. The woman was placed in the burial chamber in the aft section of the ship. Next to her lay the body of another woman, possibly a servant, as well as her most valuable possessions. Under the ship was a bed of blue clay, while the mound itself was built up of turf. This clay preserved the ship for over 1000 years.

The ship has 15 pairs of oar holes, which means that 30 people could row the ship. Other fittings include a broad steering oar, iron anchor, gangplank and a bailer. The bow and the stern of the ship are elaborately decorated with complex woodcarvings in the characteristic "gripping beast" style, also known as the Oseberg style. Although seaworthy, the ship is relatively frail, and it is thought to have been used in calm waters for pleasure sailing.

were burned on dry land. Afterward, other Vikings would place stones and soil on top of the burned remains.

OTHER EXPLORERS SAIL TO VINLAND

The next trip to Vinland was led by one of Leif's brothers, Thorvald. Around 1004, Thorvald, using Leif's ship, sailed to Vinland. He used what remained of Leif's old camp. The first summer, Thorvald and his crew explored the land to the west of Leifsbudir. His crew, however, met American Indians, probably the Algonquin. The Norse Greenlanders called them the Skraelings, meaning "Screamers." One day, Thorvald and his men came upon nine Skraelings sleeping under canoes. Thorvald and his men killed all but one of the Skraelings. The man escaped and later, many Skraelings returned to attack the settlers.

One of many arrows struck Thorvald. While he was dying, he asked his crew to bury him in Vinland. He also asked that they place a cross at his head and feet. Thorvald may have been the first European to have died and been buried in North America.[9] The crew stayed in Vinland for the winter, but in the spring, they went back to Greenland.

The sagas tell us about the next Viking expedition to Vinland. Leif's brother Thorstein wanted to go to Vinland to bring Thorvald's body back to Greenland for a proper burial. Unfortunately, his ship ran into a summer of storms and he never did get to Vinland. He went back to Greenland and died in an epidemic that winter.

The need for timber and other resources to support Greenland caused another effort to settle in Vinland. This voyage sailed in the summer of 1009.[10] Thorfinn Karlsefni, who had married the wife of Thorvald, headed this expedition. Thorfinn brought with him about 250 settlers.

At first, the Skraelings traded with Thorfinn's men. The trading was limited to cheese, milk, and cloth. For unknown reasons, the Skraelings got sick. They attacked the settlement. Thorfinn realized he could not live peacefully in their land and he returned to Greenland. His son, Snorri, was the first Norse baby to be born in Vinland.

Leif's sister, Freydis, and her husband, Thorvard, made the fourth and last-known expedition to Vinland. They became partners with two merchants, Helgi and Finnbogi, who had their own ship. Because Freydis was greedy and wanted the products her partners' collected, she made up a story, which caused Thorvard to kill them. No one would kill the women who were with the merchants, so Freydis took an ax and killed all five of them herself.[11]

As far as today's historians know, this ended the chapter of Norse history in North America, as Europe did not learn about this new world for hundreds of years.

For five centuries, people believed Columbus discovered America. Starting in 1960, archaeologists found ruins of what may have been Leif's settlement, L'Anse aux Meadows. After 2,400 Viking objects were uncovered, there is no longer any doubt that the Vikings discovered America long before Christopher Columbus. Many feel that these ruins are the remains of Leif's settlement.

WHY DID VINLAND PERISH?

The *Saga of the Greenlanders* and the *Saga of Erik the Red* tell of the discovery and settlement of Vinland. They also give possible reasons why the settlement of Vinland did not survive. Many historians feel that perhaps there were too few people to keep a settlement going, and that the settlers were homesick for friends and relatives in Greenland. Some historians, as well as the Viking sagas, suggest that there were fights among the settlers, which caused conflicts. In addition, there were problems with the American Indians, probably the Algonquin tribe.

The American Indians were the authentic discoverers of North America. Although they had been living on the continent for many thousands of years, Leif's discovery is important. It was the first known meeting between Europeans and the American Indians. However, nothing further came of this contact and North America remained closed to Europeans until the voyages of Columbus in 1492.

According to a Parks Canada archaeologist named Dr. Birgitta Wallace, "Whether these are traces of the settlements mentioned in the sagas, or from other journeys which we have no record of, it is impossible to say. However the finds [at L'Anse Aux Meadows] prove that Nordic [Viking] seafarers really sailed to the North American Continent around the year 1000." The evidence proves that the area was settled five hundred years before Christopher Columbus stepped foot on North American soil. Leif Eriksson is the first explorer of Norwegian heritage to receive worldwide recognition for his discovery of North America.

Chapter 5

VIKING CONTRIBUTIONS

The Vikings are thought of by many people as the first rcal pirates of the seas, but they should also be considered as merchants, explorers and shipbuilders. In spite of the fact that they raided and robbed settlements across Europe in the ninth and tenth centuries, they are also responsible for many important and positive contributions to life during the Viking Age and after.

Vikings deserve credit for designing ships that could cross the ocean successfully, making it possible for the discovery and exploration of distant lands by Leif Eriksson and other explorers. Vikings depended on their ships for exploring far-off lands and trading with other cultures. As a result, the Vikings became expert shipbuilders, developing ships that were able to navigate shallow rivers and the widest oceans even in poor weather conditions. Their ships looked like open canoes with a sail; they could cross the oceans under sail or switch to oars for fast hit-and-run raiding attacks on towns.

The Vikings designed two main types of ships. The drekar, or dragon-headed

Mare germanicus

In this painting entitled "Guests from Overseas" by Nicholas Roerich, a knarr or ocean-going cargo vessel is depicted.

longship, was a fast-moving warship and troop carrier. It could carry warriors, supplies, and horses on long voyages. The Vikings' design of the keels and the sleek hull helped the longship glide over the water. Because it needed only a shallow depth of water to float the ship, it could maneuver in harbors and rivers with little water.

Longships were not the only type of ships designed by the Vikings. The merchants used a ship called a *knarr,* which was an ocean-going cargo vessel. This was a slower ship than the long-ship and could carry cargo, men, and livestock across the seas.[1] The knarr allowed the Vikings to develop trading networks, which led to the coloni-zation of Iceland, Greenland, and North America. Without their key advances in ship technology, the Vikings would never have become a leading force in warfare, politics, and trade.

NAVIGATION INSTRUMENTS

Vikings were also responsible for some of our present-day navigational designs, which came from instruments developed and used by Viking explorers. Vikings were exceptional sailors. They developed many navigational instruments for plotting the courses of their ships. One of their designs was a sun board that helped keep track of the ship's route in the middle of the day. This instrument measured the height of the sun. If the angle of the sun was too big, the ship was on a southerly course. If the angle was too small, it had sailed too far north. Making a course change on the open sea could be risky. Just a small change could result in being far off course and getting lost or shipwrecked.

Vikings were also excellent navigators. They watched the sun throughout the year and knew the sun's path through the sky for every season. They determined the height of the sun for the whole year along with all the sunrises and sunsets. This information allowed a navigator to find the area on the horizon where the sun set and where it rose. The information and measurements were placed on a semi-wheel to find the four directions: north, east, south, and west and calculate the latitude.[2] People who lived in Leif's time benefited from his expeditions. His explorations made them aware of the possibilities of a new life in a new land. His expeditions helped create more trade routes between the older developed countries and new lands. Before 1300, ships from Norway and other European countries brought items to Greenland, such as timber, iron, corn, and salt. By way of a barter system, the Greenlanders traded butter, cheese, wool, and frieze cloth, a shaggy woolen cloth.[3] Greenland had items to trade that Europeans desired. These items included the skins of polar bears, walrus skins, the fur from white and blue foxes, and the tusks of walrus and narwhal.[4]

HONOR, FREEDOM, AND THE LAW

The Vikings believed deeply in honor and personal freedom. They would rather leave their homeland than accept something they did not believe was right. For instance, when King Olaf of Norway attempted to force the people of Greenland to accept Christianity as their religion, many Green-landers fled to Iceland rather than give up their pagan beliefs.

The Vikings believed in the word of the law and required that all men should obey the laws. If a dispute occurred, they looked to the Althing, their legislative body, for a ruling. In most cases, Vikings honored the findings of the Althing and accepted its decisions.

CULTURE AND TRADITIONS

The Vikings brought their culture, traditions, and beliefs to the new lands that they conquered and settled. Some new ideas from other cultures, such as Christianity, came back to the homeland as well. Throughout the Viking Age, they established a large trading network and commercial centers for trading. Building towns, shipbuilding, naviga-tion, and farming techniques were some of the skills they shared with the rest of the world. The Vikings created lasting societies in both Iceland and Greenland.

The Vikings integrated themselves so well into the life of the British Isles that many of their words have entered the English language. Because of the Vikings, English includes nouns such as *egg, knife, window, husband, fellow,* and *sister;* adjectives such as *happy, dirty,* and *ill*; and verbs such as *take, snort, want, get,* and *berserk*. A number of our weekdays are named for Viking gods: Wednesday is named for Odin (sometimes spelled Woden), and Thursday is for Thor.

The influence of Leif and the descendants of Nordic-American heritage have contributed to the United States of America in the fields of business, politics, the arts, education, agriculture, and other fields.

Chapter 6

Recognition of Leif Eriksson's Accomplishments

In the United States, Leif Eriksson's accomplishments are acknowledged and celebrated in many ways. On May 10, 1929, Governor Walter Kohler of Wisconsin signed a bill for Wisconsin to become the first state to create a Leif Eriksson Day, October 9, due to the efforts of a Norwegian-American, Rasmus B. Anderson. Two years later, in 1931, Minnesota also created a Leif Eriksson Day.

In 1964, Congress authorized President Lyndon B. Johnson to proclaim October 9 "Leif Eriksson Day."[1] This date had nothing to do with any event in Leif's life, but choosing this particular date was no accident. On October 9, 1825, *Restauration*, a ship sailing from Stavanger, Norway, arrived in New York. This marked the beginning of the first organized emigration of people from Norway to the United States.

To honor Leif Eriksson, on October 9, 1968, the U.S. Postal System issued a Leif Eriksson stamp. There was also a "2000 Leif Eriksson Millennium Commemorative Coin" minted in honor of this great explorer.

The "2000 Leif Eriksson Millennium Commemorative Coin" minted in honor of this great explorer.

The United States has its Columbus Day and its Leif Eriksson Day. The American school textbooks of today discuss the discovery of America from a very different angle than they did years ago. Now textbooks state that first came the American Indians, then the Scandinavians about the year 1000, and, finally, Christopher Columbus in 1492.[2]

The Monument of Emigration

The United States gave the people of Reykjavik, Iceland, a statue of Leif Eriksson in 1930. The statue honored the one thousandth anniversary of Althing, the Icelandic legislature.[3] On July 23, 1997, a statue of Leif Eriksson was unveiled at a ceremony in the city of Trondheim, Norway.[4] An important feature of the Trondheim statue, called *The Monument of Emigration*, is the connection between North America and the Scandinavian countries, Norway, Sweden, and Denmark. The statue contains more than five hundred names of Scandinavian families who had emigrated from Scandinavia to the Seattle, Washington, area.

In 2000, a celebration marked Leif's one hundredth anniversary sail from the harbor in Trondheim, Norway, to North America. At the celebration, five hundred more names of immigrants were presented to be added to the Trondheim statue.

Honoring a Great Explorer

The first statue of Leif Eriksson was unveiled in Boston in 1887. It became a symbol of a bond between America and Scandinavia. Three people sponsored the first statue. They were Rasmus Anderson, a professor from Wisconsin; Ole Bull, a

LEIF ERIKSSON'S MEMORIALS AND STATUES

- Boston, Massachusetts: A statue in 1887
- Chicago, Illinois: A museum in 1893; a statue in 1901
- New York: Leif Eriksson Park with a plaque made by August Werner in the 1930s
- Newport News, Virginia: A statue in 1938
- St. Paul, Minnesota: A statue in 1949
- Duluth, Minnesota: A park in 1929; a statue in 1956
- Seattle, Washington: A statue by August Werner in 1962; moved to a new location in Washington in 2007
- Sioux City, South Dakota: A statue in the 1970s
- Saskatoon, Canada: A statue in the 1970s
- L'Anse-Aux Meadows, Newfoundland, Canada: A museum of "Leif's houses" in the 1980s
- Newport News, Rhode Island: A statue in the 1990s
- Minot, North Dakota: A statue in 1994
- Trondheim, Norway: A statue in 1997
- Eiriksstadir, Iceland: A statue in 2000
- Brattahlid (Qassiarsuk), Greenland: A statue in 2000
- Cleveland, Ohio: A bust of Leif Eriksson in 2001
- Seattle, Washington: A bust of Leif Erikson by August Werner in 2003

A statue of Leif Eriksson
in Reykjavik, Iceland

Painting entitled "Leif Eriksson discovers America" by Christian Krohg. Unlike Herjolfsson, Eriksson and his men made landfall in North America.

world-famous violinist; and Eben Norton Horsford, an educator from Harvard University.

Anderson got the idea for a statue in 1869. Ole Bull had probably not heard of Eriksson before he met Anderson. However, when Ole Bull moved to Boston in 1876, the Eriksson campaign became his passion and a memorial committee was established. Of the fifty-four committee members, Rasmus

Anderson, Ole Bull, and Horsford were the leaders. Without them, the first statue of Leif Eriksson in America would not have become a reality in 1887.[5]

In the year 1893, the "Gokstad ship," a replica of a Viking longboat found at Gokstad, Norway, sailed across the Atlantic Ocean from Norway to New York, then continued on the Erie Canal and the Great Lakes to reach Chicago, Illinois. The longboat was exhibited at the World's Columbian Exposition held in Chicago. The purpose of the trip was to prove that an original Viking ship could have made the journey to Vinland from Norway.

Christian Krohg created the famous painting, *Leif Erikson Discovers America,* for the Chicago World's Columbian Exposition. The painting shows Erikkson discovering North America. Presently, this very large 9 by 18 feet (274 by 548.6 cm) painting hangs in the National Gallery in Oslo.

Many Americans and Americans of Nordic birthright are proud of Leif Eriksson and his accomplishments. As an example of American pride, in 1893, Chicago built a museum honoring the Vikings. Then in 1901, Chicago unveiled a statue of Leif. From coast to coast in the United States as well as in Norway, Iceland, and Greenland, Leif Eriksson memorials and statues stand as a tribute to this courageous explorer.

● SOME INTERESTING VIKING FRAUDS AND HOAXES

Viking history in North America is sketchy because there are no written records. But after people learned that there is proof that the Vikings did travel to the New World, frauds and hoaxes about the Vikings began to surface. The early twentieth century saw attempts to join the Vikings to people in North America or Mexico. For example, the legend of Quetzalcoatl, the great white Mexican god, linked the god with the Vikings.

There have been claims about some items and their connection to the Vikings. For instance, in 1957, a Norse penny, which was minted between 1065 and 1080, was found near Brooklin, Maine. Could this coin have come from a later Viking expedition? Over the years it was rumored that Newport Tower in Rhode Island was of Viking origin. However, in 1992, a radiocarbon dating test on the tower's mortar determined that the tower was built between 1635 and 1698.

Another artifact, the "Kensington Stone," is a stone slab that was uncovered in 1989 on a farm in Minnesota. The slab, covered in runes, is thought to be fake. Another hoax was a story about Norumbega, a fort and city that Leif Eriksson was supposed to have settled on the shores of the Charles River in Cambridge, Massachusetts. This city never existed.

Kensington Runestone

Also thought to possibly be a hoax and/or a forgery is the Vinland map, found in a medieval book in a library at Yale University in 1950. Based on the parchment used, it might have been drawn in the 1400s. Scientists and historians think that if the map is authentic, it may be the first map showing North America. Some of the text on the map reads: "By God's will, after a long voyage from the island of Greenland to the south toward the most distant remaining parts of the western ocean sea, sailing southward amidst the ice, the companions Bjarni and Leif Eiriksson discovered a new land, extremely fertile and even having vines, which island they named Vinland."

How far did Leif Eriksson's exploration take him in the New World? Is it possible that more Viking artifacts will be unearthed in the future to prove that Vikings traveled farther than we now believe? Just as it took many centuries to prove without any doubt that the Vikings reached the North American continent, it could take a long time to prove that they successfully traveled even farther.

CREDIT FOR THE VIKINGS

In addition to introducing Christianity to the people of Greenland, the Vikings deserve credit for many other important contributions. They discovered new lands, inspired shipbuilders to build ocean-going ships for exploration, and designed instruments that are used in present-day ship navigation. Viking explorations also helped to open up new trade routes and develop business and commerce with other countries.

How do we know about the Vikings' contributions? Although there are no written records such as maps, charts, or guidebooks to tell us, there are sagas, the oral stories that recount the Vikings' lives and accomplishments. The stories lived on because people listened to them. For hundreds of years, Norsemen and women listened to the tales of Naddod the Viking, Erik the Red, and Leif Eriksson. Because these stories explained the history of the Norse people, the storytellers were careful to repeat the stories as accurately as they could and include a wealth of detail. The Vikings passed their history, laws, and religion by word of mouth. No written proof from Leif's lifetime exists to prove this. Whether there were other explorers who sailed to North America before Leif is still unknown.

It may have taken a long time to find the physical proof, but many scholars give the credit for discovering North America to a Viking explorer named Leif Eriksson, who can rightfully claim his place among other world-famous explorers.

EXPLORER TIMELINE

During Leif Eriksson's lifetime, most people could not read or write. As a result, history was not recorded until many years, sometimes hundreds of years, after an event had happened. Because no one knows for sure the exact date when something really occurred during this period, written sources often give a range using words such as "about, between, or around."

Around A.D. 750—The Viking Age begins.

Around A.D. 950—"Erik the Red," Leif Eriksson's father, is born in Norway.

Around A.D. 960—Thorvald Asvaldsson, Eriksson's grandfather, is banished from Norway for committing murder. He takes his son, Erik the Red, and moves to Iceland.

Between A.D. 975 and A.D. 985—Leif Eriksson is born in Iceland.

Between 980 and 986—Leif moves to Greenland with his family.

At age twenty-four, Leif becomes captain of his own ship and sets sail to deliver gifts to King Olaf Tryggvason of Norway. On his way to Norway, Leif is blown off course.

Leif meets a woman named Thorgunna in the Hebrides Islands. She gives birth to Leif's only child, Thorkell.

Around A.D. 1000—Leif is commissioned by King Olaf to convert the settlers in Greenland to Christianity.

Between A.D. 1000 and A.D. 1003—Leif sets sail to find the land that Bjarni Herjulfsson had seen to the west of Greenland. First Eriksson discovers Helluland, probably Baffin Island.

His second discovery is Markland, probably Labrador, Canada. His third discovery is Vinland, most likely the northern tip of Newfoundland, Canada.

Leif returns to Greenland from North America and rescues fifteen people who are shipwrecked. Between the reward for the rescue, his cargo, and the cargo from the rescued ship, Leif becomes a very rich man and is called "Leif the Lucky."

Around A.D. **1003**—Eric the Red dies. Leif becomes the Paramount Chieftain in Greenland and inherits his father's estate, Brattahlid.

Between A.D. **1020 and** A.D. **1025**—Leif Eriksson dies.

Around A.D. **1100**—The Viking Age ends.

Around A.D. **1200**—The first sagas are written.

Around A.D. **1410**—The Viking settlement in Greenland ends after 400 years when the last ship leaves the colony and sails for Norway

Chapter 1: Who Discovered North America?

1. "Viking Voyage—National Museum of Natural History—Smithsonian Institute." n.d. <http://www.mnh.si.edu/Vikings/voyage/defin.html> (April 12, 2008).

2. Ibid.

3. Ibid.

4. Michael Lemonick and Andrea Dorfman, "The Amazing Vikings," *Time Magazine Europe* vol. 155, no. 20. (May 22, 2000) <http://www.time.com/time/europe/magazine/2000/0522/cover.html> (November 5, 2009).

5. Ibid.

6. Donald F. Logan, *The Vikings in History*, Second Edition (Taylor & Francis e-Library, 2003), p. 97.

7. Ibid., p. 99.

8. "Parks Canada-History" L'Anse aux Meadows National Historic Site of Canada. n.d.<http://www.pc.gc.ca/lhn-nhs/nl/meadows/natcul/decouverte_discovery.aspx1> (November 5, 2009).

9. Michael Lemonick and Andrea Dorfman, "The Amazing Vikings," *Time Magazine Europe* vol. 155, no. 20. (May 22, 2000) http://www.time.com/time/europe/magazine/2000/0522/cover.html (October 5, 2009).

10. Following the Viking Trail, Day 6. http://www.travelblog.org/North_America/Canada/Newfoundland—Labrador/L'Anse-aux (April 9, 2009).

11. "Parks Canada-History" L'Anse aux Meadows National Historic Site of Canada. *Viking Encampment: 1000 AD* (April 24, 2009)<http://www.pc.gc.ca/eng/rech-srch/clic-click.aspx?/cgi-bin/MsmGo.exe?grab_id=0&page_id=14903&query=radiocarbon%20dating%20L%20Anse%20aux%20Meadows&hiword=ANSER%20ANSES%20Anse%20L%20MEADOW%20Meadows%20

R A D I O C A R B O N E % 2 0 a u x % 2 0 d a t i n g % 2 0 radiocarbon%20>(November 5, 2009).

12. "GORP" L'Anse aux Meadows Historic Site' <http://gorp.away.com/gorp/location/canada/ newfoundland/viking.htm (April 12, 2009).

Chapter 2: Leif Eriksson's Family Tree

1. "Leif Eriksson's Family Tree," Donald F. Logan, *The Vikings in History* (Taylor & Francis e-Library, 2003), p. 74.

2. Kristine, Axelsdottir. "The Discovery of Iceland." *The Viking Network Info-Sheet*. n.d. p. 1. <http://www. viking.no/e/info-sheets/iceland/iceland.htm> (October 23, 2007).

3. David Arter Scandinavian Politics Today (Manchester, England: Manchester University Press, 1999) p. 12.

4. Scott A. Mandia, "Vikings During the Medieval Warm Period." n.d. <http://www2.sunysuffolk.edu/ mandias/lia/vikings_during_mwp.html> (April 30, 2008).

5. Ibid.

6. Ibid.

7. Todd B. Krause and Jonathan Slocum, *Old Norse Online* (May 13, 2009)<http://www.utexas.edu/cola/ centers/lrc/eieol/norol-0-X.html>(November 5, 2009)

8. Ibid.

9. Ibid.

10. Carolyn Tytler, *Leif Ericson and the Discovery of North America* (August 24, 2009) <http://www .associatedcontent.com/article/2101451/leif_ericson_ and_the_discovery_of_north.html> (November 5, 2009)

11. Ibid.

12. Charles C. Rafn, "Leif Ericson Discovers America" <http://history-world.org/leif_ericson_discovers_ america.htm> (November 5, 2009).

13. Ibid.

14. Ibid.

15. James Graham-Campbell, *The Viking World*, Third Edition. (London: Frances Lincoln, Ltd., 2001) p. 82.

16. "Where is Vinland?" Leif Eiriksson, "Leif the Lucky" n.d. <http://www.canadianmysteries.ca/sites/vinland/whereisvinland/leif/indexen.html> (November 5, 2009).

17. Rachel Bellerby, *Viking Weapons—Weaponry used by the Vikings in War, Sea Battles and Raids*, (April 14, 2008), http://early-middle-ages.suite101.com/article.cfm/viking_weapons> (November 5, 2009)

18. "Hurstwic: Viking Helmets" http://www.hurstwic.org/history/articles/manufacturing/text/Viking_helmets.htm> pg. 1 (November 5, 2009).

Chapter 3: Leif Eriksson's First Voyage

1. "Leif Eriksson's First Voyage" Great Unsolved Mysteries in Canadian History: Where is Vineland? Leif Eriksson in 'Eirik the Red's Saga', Chapter 5" <http://www.canadianmysteries.ca/sites/vinland/whereisvinland/leif/3843en.htm> (November 5, 2009).

2. "Greenland-Church of Tjodhilde in Brattahilid-Official Greenland Travel Guide" n.d. <http://www.greenland.com/content/english/tourist/culture/the-history-of-greenland> (November 5, 2009).

3. D. L. Ashman, "Iceland Accepts Christianity" abstracted from Njal's Saga, (February 19, 2001) <http://www.pitt.edu/~dash/njal100.html> (November 5, 2009).

Chapter 4: A Major Discovery

1. "A Major Discovery" *Modern History Sourcebook: Discovery of North America by Leif Ericsson, c. 1000 from The Saga of Eric the Red*, 1387. p. 2. March 2, 2009.

2. Gwen Jones. *A History of the Vikings* (New York: Oxford University Press, 2001) p. 298.

3. Donald F. Logan, *The Vikings in History*, Second Edition (Taylor & Francis e-Library, 2003), p. 97.

4. The American Museum of Natural History "Vikings—The North Atlantic Saga: The Sagas II: Leif Eriksson" n.d. <http://www.amnh.org/exhibitions/vikings/saga2.html> (November 5, 2009).

5. Rachel Bellerby, *The Viking Longhouse: How People Lived in the Viking Age*, (April 27, 2009), http://early-middle-ages.suite101.com/article.cfm/the_viking_longhouse> (November 5, 2009).

6. "Where is Vinland?" Leif Eiriksson, "Leif the Lucky" n.d. <http://www.canadianmysteries.ca/sites/vinland/whereisvinland/leif/indexen.htm> (November 5, 2009).

7. Paul Halsall, *Modern History Sourcebook: The Discovery of North America by Leif Ericsson, c. 1000 from The Saga of Eric the Red, 1387*, (August, 1998) <http://www.fordham.edu/halsall/mod/1000Vinland.html> (November 5, 2009)

8. Ibid.

9. "Where is Vinland?" Thorvald Eirikssonn n.d. <http://www.canadianmysteries.ca/sites/vinland/whereisvinland/thorvald/indexen.html> (November 5, 2009).

10. "Where is Vineland?" p. 3 <http://www.canadianmysteries.ca/sites/vinland/whereisvinland/sagaofgreenlanders/indexen> (November 5, 2009).

11. "The Norse Discovery of America: Book 1. Arguments and Proofs That Support the Claim—The Saga of Eric The Red." Thorrstein Ericsson Weds Gudrid; Apparitions. nd. pg. 47 <http://www.sacred-texts.com/neu/nda/nda06.htm> (May 17, 2008).

Chapter 5: Viking Contributions

1. Scott A. Mandia, "Vikings During the Medieval Warm Period" n.d. <http://www2.sunysuffolk.edu/mandias/lia/vikings_during_mwp.html> (April 30, 2008).

2. "Navigation Instruments." *The Viking Network*. April 15, 2000. <http://www.viking.no/e/travels/navigation/e-instru.htm> (October 11, 2007).

3. Mandia.

4. Ibid.

Chapter 6: Recognition of Leif Eriksson's Accomplishments

1. "Leif Erikson Day, 2007." *The White House*. October 4, 2004 <http://www.whitehouse.gov/news/releases/2004/10/20071004-2.html>(November 5, 2009).

2. Rolf Grankvist. (Dean Emeritus of the School of Education and History Professor, Trondheim University, Norway.) "The Monument of Emigration" *Pamphlet from Trondheim Port Authority*. n.d.

3. David Arter, *Scandinavian Politics Today* (Manchester, England: Manchester University Press, 1999) p. 225.

4. "Trondheim: Eriksson Monument" <http://leiferiksson.vanderkrogt.net/files/trondheim.html> (May 30, 2009).

5. Rolf Grankist.

Glossary

Althing—The national legislative body of Iceland; the governing assembly that is made up of the free people in the community.

archaeology—The study of historic people and their cultures.

artifacts—Handmade objects belonging to an earlier time or culture.

banish—To cast out or exile a person from a country.

barbarians—People whose behavior is considered uncivilized.

Brattahlid—The Greenland estate of Erik the Red and later Leif Eriksson.

emigrate—To go from one country to another in order to settle there.

exile—To send a person away from his or her country or home as a punishment.

explorer—A person who investigates unknown regions.

fjord—A long, narrow inlet of the sea between cliffs or steep slopes.

invasion—A hostile entry into a territory with the intention to overrun or conquer it.

knots—Measurement of the speed of a ship or boat; one nautical mile per hour.

monastery—A religious building where monks live.

monks—Men who live in a religious community and devote their lives to prayer and religion.

navigation—Plotting and directing a ship's course.

Old Norse—The North Germanic language of the Scandinavian people, which was spoken by people during the Viking Age.

outlaw—A criminal or lawbreaker who does not have the protection of the law.

pagans—People who do not believe in Christianity, Judaism, or Islam.

pillage—To rob with force and open violence.

runes—The old Germanic alphabet used between the third and thirteenth centuries.

sagas—Detailed Scandinavian oral stories repeated over time about historical or legendary events in the lives of people.

skerry—A small offshore rocky island.

snowfield—Glaciers begin in a snowfield; an extensive area covered by snow.

thrall—A slave in the culture during the Viking Age.

turf—The upper part of soil bound by grass and plant roots into a thick mat.

Viking—A member of a people who lived in Norway, Sweden, Denmark, and Iceland. The Vikings built ships, raided the coasts of Europe, and voyaged to North America during the eighth to eleventh centuries.

Viking Age—A term for the years from about A.D. 700 to 1066 in Scandinavian history.

whetstone—A stone used to sharpen blades on weapons and tools.

Further Reading

Berger, Gilda. *The Real Vikings: Craftsmen, Traders, and Fearsome Raiders*. Washington, D.C.: National Geographic Children's Books, 2003.

Freedman, Russell. *Who Was First?: Discovering the Americas.* New York : Clarion Books, 2007.

Graham-Campbell, James. *Viking World.* London: Frances Lincoln Ltd. 2001

Logan, Donald F. *The Vikings in History*. New York: Routledge, 2005.

Margeson, Susan M. *Viking.* London: New York: DK, 2005.

Rice, Earle Jr. *Leif Eriksson.* Mitchell Lane Publishers. 2008. New York: Children's Press, 2001.

Schomp, Virginia. *The Vikings.* New York: Children's Press, 2005.

Stefoff, Rebecca. *Exploring the New World.* Tarrytown, N.Y.: Benchmark Books, 2001.

INTERNET ADDRESSES

Great Unsolved Mysteries in Canadian History, "Where is Vinland?"
<http://www.canadianmysteries.ca/sites/vinland/home/aboutthissite/indexen.html>

The Smithsonian Institution, National Museum of Natural History, "Vikings: The North Atlantic Saga"
<http://www.mnh.si.edu/vikings/start.html>

NOVA OnLine: Who Were the Vikings?
<http://www.pbs.org/wgbh/nova/vikings/who.html>

Index